Paris Sketchbook

Rue Condorcet 2003
Pencil 6" x 4" (15 x 10cms)

Aspects of the City

Philip James Studio

Cv / Visual Arts Research Series 22

PARIS SKETCHBOOK
Aspects of the City

ISBN 978-1-908419-43-9
ISSN 1476-9980

Monograph copyright © 2004/2012 Cv Publications
Images and texts Copyright © Philip James Studio

The right of N.P. James to be identified as the author of this
work has been asserted in accordance with sections 77 and 78
of the Copyright, Designs and Patents Act 1988

All rights reserved; no part of this publication may be stored in a retrieval system, or
transmitted in any form or by any means, electronic, mechanical, photocopying, recording,
or otherwise, without the prior written permission of the Publishers.

Except in the United States of America, this book is sold subject to the condition that it shall not,
by way of trade or otherwise be lent, re-sold, hired out, or otherwise circulated without the
publisher's prior consent in any form of binding other than that in which it is published and
without a similar condition including this condition being imposed on the subsequent publisher.

The second printing in July 2012
Printed and bound by
Blissett: Design.Print.Media
www.blissettdigital.co.uk

Cv Publications
The Barley Mow Centre,
10, Barley Mow Passage,
London W4 4PH
www.tracksdirectory.ision.co.uk

Paris Sketchbook

'Paris provides constant stimulation; the city remains a fabulous animal, volatile, individualist and alive with its history and possibilities.'

For his new cityscapes N.P.James made an artistic investigation of Paris, walking through the various districts of Opera, St.Lazare, Republic, Montmartre, Montparnasse, Le Marais, St. Denis and St.Germain. His sketchbook records aspects of the streets, buildings, courtyards and monuments, in a web of small pencil drawings, which underpinned the paintings. Colour photographs, notes and observations of the historic and fabled city accompany the studies.

Nicholas Philip James studied Painting (BA) with Frank Auerbach and Keith Vaughan at the Slade School of Art. His primary attraction to landscape developed in works made on site in Sussex, Devon, Cornwall and the Lake District leading to city series of London and Paris. He regularly exhibits at The Royal Society of Oil Painters (Elected ROI in 2006). His work is held in numerous collections in England and America.

Itineraries 2003/2005

10/01/2003
Republic - Opera
Gare Du Nord
Rue La Fayette
Rue Faubourg Montmartre
Rue Richer
Rue Saulmer
Rue De Trevise
Rue De Faubourg
Poissonière
Rue Des Petits Ecuries
Rue Du Faubourg St Denis
Rue d'Enghière
Rue De Metz
Boulevard St Denis
Place Johann Strauss
Place De La Republique
Cité Du Vauxhall
Boulevard De Magenta
Rue Des Vinaigres
Rue De Chabrol

11/01/2003
Montmartre - St Germain -
Le Marais
Rue De Menthalon
Rue Du Faubourg
Montmartre
Boulevard Poissonière
Rue Notre Dames
Des Victoires
Rue Montmartre
Rue Réaumùr
Rue Léopold Bellan
Rue d'Argout
Rue Etienne Marcell
Rue Du Jour
Rue Rambuteau
Rue St Eustache

Rue De Pont Neuf
Pont Neuf
Quai Des Grands Augustins
Rue Dauphin
Rue Mazarine
Rue De Seine
Boulevard St Germain
RRue Mabillon
Rue Garangiere
Rue De Vaugirard
Rue Corneille
Rue Notre Dame
Rue De Rivoli
Place De La Bastille
Boulevard Beaumarchais
Rue St Gilles
Rue De Temple
Rue De Turennes
Rue De Bretagne
Rue De Chabrol

12/01/2003
St.Lazare - Concorde - Les Halles
Rue De Mauberge
Rue Lamartine
Rue de Chateaudun
Boulevard Haussmann
Rue d'Anjou
Boulevard Malherbes
Rue Faubourg St Honoré
Rue Royale
Place De La Concorde
Avenue Franklin D.Roosevelt
Rue Jean Goujon
Champs Elysées
Quai Des Tuileries
Quai Du Louvre
Les Halles

13/01/2003
Pigalle - Sacre Coeur
Rue Pierre Senard
Rue De Mauberge
Rue Condorcet
Rue De Rochechouart
Rue Des Martyrs
Boulevard De Clichy
Rue Lepic
Rue Les Abbesses
Rue Tholoze
Rue Norvins
Rue St Rustique
Rue Poulbot
Rue Paul Albert
Rue De Gilgnancourt
Rue Christiane
Boulevard Barbes

14/01/2003
Clichy - Arc De Triomphe - St Lazare
Boulevard De Clichy
Boulevard De Batignolles
Rue De Rome
Boulevard Des Courcelles
Avenue Foche
Avenue De Friedland
Rue De La Pepiniere
Place Kossuth
Rue La Fayette
Gare Du Nord
Boulevard Des Courcelles
Avenue Fôche
Avenue De Friedland

20/08/-21.08.2005
Chatelet . St.Chapelle
Blvd St Michel .
Les Jardins De Luxembourg .
Montparnasse
Rue Vaugirard
Rue Montmartre
Montparnasse
Rue Vaugirard
Blvd St Germain
Chatelet Les Halles
.

21/08/2005
Chatelet
St.Chapelle
Blvd St Michel
Les Jardins de Luxembourg
Montparnasse
Rue Vaugirard
Blvd St Germain
Chatelet Les Halles
Rue Montmartre
Blvd Montmartre .

22/08/2005
Rouen
Les Jardins deTuilerie
St Germain Des Pres
23.08.05 Rue De Rivoli

Rue Richer The long narrow lane of a run down quarter leading of the Rue La Fayette. Fur and leather shops, shoes, electrical supplies. Rue Richer includes the Folies Bergères with its great 1930s deco frontage.

Rue Du Jour
Pencil 6″ x 4″ (15 x 10cms)

Rue Du Jour 2
Pencil 6″ x 4″ (15 x 10cms)

Boulevard St Martine A schoolgirl drops her satchel and retrieves it laughing and runs on. A woman with a yellow and black striped scarf wound about her head and draped over a long fur coat waits hesitantly at the junction.

Store Construction, Rue De Pont Neuf
Pencil 6″ x 4″ (15 x 10cms)

Rue Mazarin
Pencil 6″ x 4″ (15 x 10cms)

Rue Mazarine
Pencil 6″ x 4″ (15 x 10cms)

Rue Dauphin
Pencil 6″x 4″ (15 x 10cms)

Rue Jacob
Pencil 6″ x 4″ (15 x 10cms)

Spitting A group of men stands on the corner of the Rue , lounging around and passing casual conversation. One of their number, sallow faced with dark curled hair, turns and spits in the path of the visitor before lighting a cigarette.

Rue Mazarin
Pencil 6"x 4" (15 x 10cms)

Rue Mabillon
Pencil 6″ x 4″ (15 x 10cms)

Rue Guisarde
Pencil 6″x 4″ (15 x 10cms)

Cemetary "Père Lachaise is too far to walk to, you must take the metro to Gambetta. I live near there at Parc des Buttes Chalments" The helpful woman in a sandwich bar points out directions on a map of the city.

St. Sulpice
Pencil 6" x 4" (15 x 10cms)

Rue De Vaugirard
Pencil 6″ x 4″ (15 x 10cms)

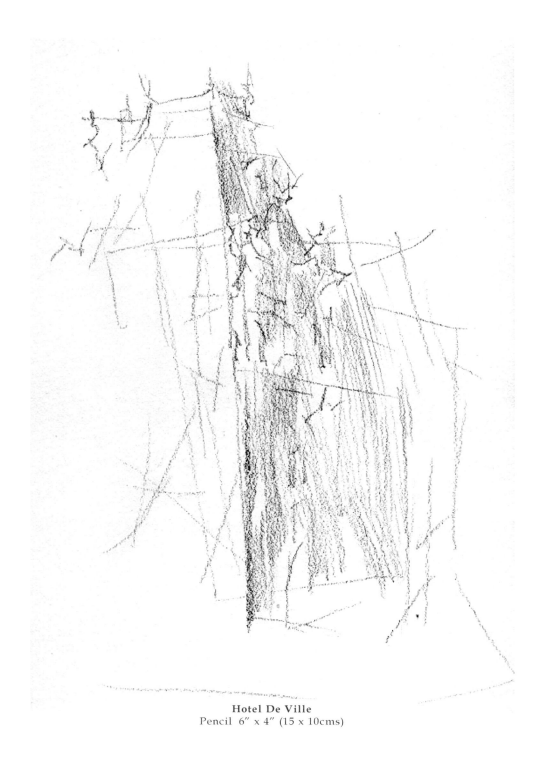

Hotel De Ville
Pencil 6″ x 4″ (15 x 10cms)

Interior, Notre Dame
Pencil 6"x 4" (15 x 10cms)

Rue De Turenne
Pencil 6″ x 4″ (15 x 10cms)

Rue Cadet Boucherie, Viandes, Charcuterie, Boulanger, Patisserie; specialist shops and full fruit stalls are still open for business late in the evening, in the Rue Cadet, off the Rue La Fayette.

Rue St Gilles
Pencil 6″ x 4″ (15 x 10cms)

Fruit Stall Plastic wrapped stacks of various brands of bottled water and pressed fruit juices. In a glass cabinet salamis, sausage and ham. Disordered packets of biscuits and cereals are piled high on shelves. The stall holder claps his hands in the bitter cold, sorting some coins of change for the customer at a small store on the Rue Cadet.

Rue De Malsherbe
Pencil 6" x 4" (15 x 10cms)

Black Water Black swathes of water flecked with foam stream from the entrance of the Quick Store in the Rue Faubourg Montmartre, as the owner cleans the doorway in early morning.

Rue De Bretagne
Pencil 6″x 4″ (15 x 10cms)

Trees, Boulevard Haussman
Pencil 6″ x 4″ (15 x 10cms)

Rue D'Anjou
Pencil 6″ x 4″ (15 x 10cms)

Rue Du Jour A man attends to his little dog as it relieves itself in the gutter of the Rue Du Jour in the quiet of early morning in the 2nd Arrondissement.

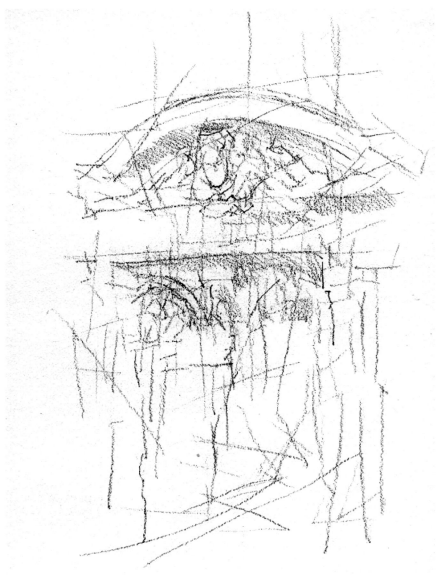

Boulevard Madeleine
Pencil 6″ x 4″ (15 x 10cms)

Notre Dame "An American coffee in Paris?" The waiter jokes with visitors in a café bar near Notre Dame. "A small Fanta?" One asks – "Small, large, it's all the same price" The waiter replies. "You can pay now, later, or never?"

Avenue Dutuit
Pencil 6"x 4" (15 x 10cms)

Hors Carré, Musée Du Louvre
Pencil 6″ x 4″ (15 x 10cms)

Eglise St Germain
Pencil 6″x 4″ (15 x 10cms)

Rue Condorcet
Pencil 6″ x 4″ (15 x 10cms)

Rue Des Martyrs
Pencil 6″x 4″ (15 x 10cms)

Rue Des Martyrs 2
Pencil 6" x 4" (15 x 10cms)

Rue De Temple A young woman with long black hair shaped in a straight fringe, wearing an ankle-length black coat and stiletto boots, talks intensely on her mobile phone, turning occasionally to regard the gridlocked traffic in the narrow lane of Rue De Temple.

Rue De Temple 2 he narrow lane of the Rue De Temple becomes completely blocked, with cars reversing and gridlocked in a battle of blaring horns. A troop of police appear, armed with revolvers and batons, chatting amiably as they march along in pairs.

Temple, Boulevard De Clichy
Pencil 6" x 4" (15 x 10cms)

Monoprix "Combien ceci?" The man enquires the price for a string of feathers."Onze euros" A girl unpacking a trolley replies." The long queue to the checkout causes too much delay so he leaves the goods on the side and exits from the crush of the sales to the street.

Rue Paul Albert
Pencil 6"x 4" (15 x 10cms)

35

Windswept An Algerian woman muffles her face with a long scarf, wound about a mass of coiled hair and dropped over the shoulder down a long fur-trimmed coat, shielding her against the sharp chill of early evening on the windswept Boulevard Magenta.

Rue Notre Dame De Lorette
Pencil 6″ x 4″ (15 x 10cms)

Sacré Coeur A notice at the gate of Moulin De La Galette records its complex history as a landmark atop the hill of Montmartre ; the turbulence of the Revolution, its attraction for artists such as Renoir and Lautrec who painted the social gatherings. Nearby in the Place du Tertre is a clutch of contemporary artists, who offer a variety of sentimental views daubed in thick texture on unframed canvases.

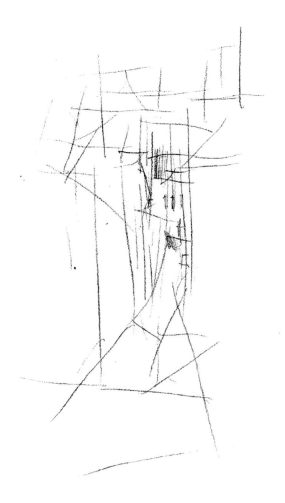

Steps from Sacré Coeur
Pencil 6″ x 4″ (15 x 10cms)

Art 'Entrée Libre', the notice scrawled on a piece of paper invites viewing of a selection of objects and artefacts in a private gallery. A bearded man settles back in the shadows by a large canvas, bare but for a black curled mark below the centre.

Moulin Rouge
Pencil 6″ x 4″ (15 x 10cms)

Dark Window In a darkened window can be discerned stacks of cartons, a scatter of lamps, filaments, torches, brackets, wire coils and batteries, in a disused electrical store in a dusty side street.

Rue De La Pepinière
Pencil 6″ x 4″ (15 x 10cms)

Pitch A beggar in the Boulevard Beaumarchais guards his pitch, muffled against the cold with swathes of blankets. His several dogs sit and lie about the broad triangle of pavement, amidst a scatter of cereal boxes and dishes of pink compressed meat, on sheaves of newspaper spread for their comfort.

Avenue De Friedland
Pencil 6"x 4" (15 x 10cms)

Crowds Crowds in the Rue St Lazare jostle each other, ferreting through street stands of bags, shoes, hats and coats. A mother pulls her crying child to the junction where fresh flows of people cross the halted traffic, under the rackety steel girders of the train line going to the Gare Du Nord.

Rue De Rome
Pencil 6" x 4" (15 x 10cms)

41

19th-23rd August 2005

Paris TV The couple exchange vows at the altar. At the moment of betrothal the bride fumbles her wedding ring which falls to the floor. As she bends to pick it up a shot rings out from an assassin. In a light comedy two men puzzle how to resolve a problem with an office lift. They are eventually joined by an attractive brunette who assists in their debate. She dreams of her lover, then meets him working as a carpenter on a house. There is an evident warmth of mutual attraction. He invites her to join him on a boat ride and they view the sunset together over the ocean. He then takes her to his home where they develop their engagement more closely.

On the night ferry crossing a woman allows an amorous engagement with a young man, after a romantic preamble their rather bony naked frames clank urgently together. A secondary bout happens in the middle of the night. In the morning they shower and dress. She then departs to meet her husband and child who wait on the quay, and drives away past the young man with a cool detached expression.

Boulevard Du Palais The Boulevard Du Palais falls silent and without movement as armed police seal either end in a security alert. Tourists drift quietly away from the scene, seeking another exit from the Isle De St Louis.

20.08.05 Place Vendôme: Arpels-Van Cleef . Chanel . Boucheron . Cartier . Bulgari . Versace . Armani

Chanel A broad built man in light slacks and blue striped shirt is accompanied by a sleek blonde some twenty years his junior, her ash hair tied back tightly, dark glasses over refined features, the immaculate image completed by an elegant black sheath dress and polished stilettoes. The glass door is opened promptly by the assistant and they are welcomed to the interior of the boutique. A Chinese tourist and his wife present themselves at the glass door of Chanel and signal a request for admission, but the assistant pointedly turns his back and faces the interior.

Faubourg St.Honoré: Dior . Yves St.Laurent . Chanel . Sotheby's . Dolce & Gabanna

Dolce & Gabanna After the visitors have checked the price of a belt (180E) The door is promptly opened to assist their prompt exit from the store.

Mme Chirac Mme Chirac guides viewer through the corridors of power adding her commentary to old clips of Pr. Mitterand at work in his administration, and to a film of the arrival of The Queen and Duke of Edinburgh on a state visit. The Royal car draws slowly to a halt at the advent of a red carpet. The visiting dignitaries are greeted by the country's leaders, and later stand in line to receive selected guests before commencing an ornate banquet of immaculate presentation. Civil servants emerge and disappear from rooms in long quiet corridors in the centre of administration. Officials gather in small groups for conversation in corners of the centre of administration.

21.08.05 Porte Glignancourt . Marché Biron . Marché Malik

Flea Market Antique dealers in Marché Biron are barely awake at 11am on Sunday morning. Their stock is less than attractive; ornate and heavy walnut desks, dressers and cupboards, edged with vulgar gold and silver scrollwork; gaudy ormulu vases and over-ripe 19th century paintings and drop chandeliers. The visitors ask for directions to the young designers based at Marché Malik, only to find a trawl of not so cheap sweat shirts, slacks and used trainers. Otherwise stalls offer broken plastic toys, suspect watches, old CDs, dog-eared paperbacks and endless racks of african beadwork and trinkets.

21.08.05 Chatelet . St.Chapelle . Blvd St Michel . Les Jardins De Luxembourg . Montparnasse . Rue Vaugirard . Blvd St Germain . Chatelet Les Halles . Rue Montmartre . Blvd Montmartre . St.Chapelle

"Shhhh – je vous en prie!" A ghostly message from speakers causes giggles among streams of chatting visitors who view the exquisite medieval stained glass windows of St.Chapelle.

Luxembourg Gardens A waiter serves several customers skilfully balancing stacks of used crockery while dispensing menus at a decorative wooden café in the Luxembourg Gardens. Visitors take their ease by a round pond, watching children and fathers play with toy boats.

Boulevard Montparnasse A man shrieks at a woman who retreats terrified into a pharmacy in Montparnasse. Security guards move towards him; he gestures madly in defiance and eventually lopes off.

Hard Rock "*Start me up!*", Mick Jagger performs staccato movements to the vigorous supporting guitar riffs of Keith Richards and Ron Wood in a Rolling Stones promo video played on multi-screens through the Hard Rock Café in the Boulevard Montmartre. The diners toy with a bowl of creamed spinach which accompanies their cheeseburger and fries. The chef curses loudly as a plate smashes to the floor, then amuses the waiting staff by performing a little ballet of recovery, scooping up chips and placing them under the hooded grill.
Taking a taxi from the restaurant the traffic slows past a swarm of armed police who have sealed the area of an incident, their warning lights flashing in the darkness. And yet again a section of the boulevard is cordoned off as the incident extends.

22.08.05 Rouen Cathedral Visitors sit on steps in front of the ornate aspect of Rouen Cathedral waiting for admission. Signboards bear information of a forthcoming Monet Spectacle, a projection of brightly colours and textures over the edifice in an entertaining light show. In 1879 the artist moved to the area, buying a large house at Giverny near Vernon. A few years later he occupied a front room above a draper's shop at no.31 on the square to realise his project of thirty paintings of the right tower of the cathedral painted at different times of the day. His ambition was to prove the material pre-eminence of light to a cathedral. Evicted by the owner he moved to a milliner's next door, setting up his easel by the ladies changing room to their intense discomfort.

Girls on a Train "Anglais? 45 euros fine normally" An inspector signals to a girl to remove her feet from the opposite seat. Two girls board at Vernon and settle down to look at images on their digi-camera and mobile phone, chattering excitedly all the way to Gare St.Lazare.

Tuilerie Gardens A strongly built woman and her partner break into a run in the Tuilerie Gardens, but the thief of her camera is quicker, speeding away through the trees to the Place De La Concorde. A security guard is half asleep as he ineffectually joins the chase.

Rue De Rivoli "The exchange rate is to your advantage" The boutique owner advises the visitor. "Paris is finished in the fashion business" She adds, "You have some very bright operators in London now. It's New York first, London second and Paris third."

Reflections of the rue de Rivoli 2005
Photograph: Lucy James

Reflections of the rue de Rivoli (detail)
Photograph: Lucy James

Reflections of the rue de Rivoli (detail)
Photograph: Lucy James

Reflections of the rue de Rivoli (detail)
Photograph: Lucy James

Reflections of the rue de Rivoli (detail)
Photograph: Lucy James

Reflections of the rue de Rivoli (detail)
Photograph: Lucy James

Reflections of the rue de Rivoli (detail)
Photograph: Lucy James

Reflections of the rue de Rivoli (detail)
Photograph: Lucy James

Rue de Temple 2003
Photograph: N.P. James

Dandyrama, Boulevard Magenta 2003
Photograph: N.P. James

Interviews

Arman
Elspeth Barratt
Nicola Bealing
Denis Bowen
Stuart Brisley
Anthony Caro
Helen Chadwick
Brian Clarke
John Cobb
Lynn Dennison
Deborah Duffin
Brian Eno
Garry Fabian Miller
Rose Garrard
David Griffiths
Leslie Hakim-Dowek
Anthea Holmes
Phillip King
John Latham
Jock McFadyen
Elizabeth Magill
Maurizio Nannucci
Hughie O'Donoghue
Glòria Ortega
Eduardo Paolozzi
Michael Porter
Rebecca Price
June Redfern
Louise Sheridan
John Skelton
Paramjit Takhar
Gérard Titus-Carmel
Amikam Toren
James Turrell
Sheila Vollmer
Rachel Whiteread
Alison Wilding
Richard Wilson

Recordings 1988-2011

Cv/VAR Archive & Editions

ISBN 978-1-905571-50-5

Interviews

2

Recordings from
Cv/VAR Archive 2010

James Aldridge
Morag Ballard
Christiane
Baumgartner
Jim Dine
Luke Frost
Rachel Goodyear
Valérie Jolly
Ansel Krut
Langlands & Bell
Christopher Le Brun
Littlewhitehead
Hew Locke
David Nash
Thérèse Oulton
Peter Randall-Page
Rob Ryan
Yinka Shonibare MBE
Christopher Stevens
Lara Viana

Artists

ISBN 978-0-956520-24-1

Albion

Dreams of the City

Circle; Whitehall Café; Queue.Top Model; Bleak House; Goddess; Prone; Little Britain; Whine; Liquid Wall; Presenter; Together; Casualty; Flashback; Fat; Tray; Greeting; Dead Land; Give; Melrose; Senior; Threshing; Poured; Captain; Signal; Drama; Spirit; Moments; Matinee; Vidal; Companion; Neighbour; Competitors; Chocolate Factory; Victor; Grazing; Detective; Reflection; Chronicler; Repeat; Casualty; The Crew; They Laugh; As If; TV Couple; Bambi; Expert; Low Life; Savants; Car Robot; Alter Ego; Fat Lips; Da Vinci Code; Visions; Crossing; Market Day; Roll; Older-Younger; Ray; Driver; The North; Pink Tie; Sign; Real; The '60s; Baby; Rebus; Britz; King and Queen; Waitress; Two Women; Borat; Dead-Not Dead; One Size

Journal

N.P.James

ISBN 978-1908419-19-4

Small
Histories

Studies of Western Art

Masaccio . Lucas Cranach . Vermeer . Velázquez . Cézanne .
Salvador Dalí . Francis Bacon . Damien Hirst . John Piper .
Vivan Sundaram . Rebecca Salter . Andrea Zittel . Yves Klein .
Sandro Chia . John Stezaker . Elisabeth Frink . Tina Modotti .
Eva Hesse . Maria Lalic . Gerhard Richter . John Baldessari .
Matthew Barney . Ruth Root . Jeff Koons . Andy Warhol

Cv/VAR Archive and Editions

ISBN 978-0-56520-27-2

Also in this series

Andy Warhol
The Most Beautiful Painting

Being Tracey
Life into Art

Lucian Freud
Mapping the Human

Helen Chadwick
Of Mutability

James Turrell
Inside Outside

David Medalla
Works in the World

Monumenta
Anish Kapoor at Grand Palais

DISTRIBUTED IN EUROPE
by
Central Books Ltd
99 Wallis Road
LONDON E9 5LN
Tel +44 [0] 20 8986 4854
Fax +44 [0] 20 8533 5821

By license to
Google Ebooks
US/CA/AU/UK/DE/ES/IT
+
Amazon Kindle Editions
US/UK/FR/DE/ES/IT

Editorial enquiries to:

Cv Publications
The Barley Mow Centre
London W4 4PH
Tel +44(0)20 8400 6160
cvpub@ision.co.uk

Title folders at:
www.tracksdirectory.ision.co.uk